This book belongs to:

Morgan....Ann....
....Lange...............

Written by Moira Butterfield
Illustrated by Rachael O'Neill

This edition published by Parragon Books Ltd in 2015
and distributed by

Parragon Inc.
440 Park Avenue South, 13th Floor
New York, NY 10016
www.parragon.com

ISBN 978-1-4748-0340-3

Printed in China

Excuse Me!

PaRragon

Bath • New York • Cologne • Melbourne • Delhi
Hong Kong • Shenzhen • Singapore • Amsterdam

Mind your child's manners!

It's important to start teaching good manners early so that they become a habit for life. The stories in the MIND YOUR MANNERS! series are written to make learning good manners a positive experience.

Here are some of the ways you can help to make it fun:

* Find a quiet time to look at this story together and encourage your child to join in. The rhymes make the story easy to remember.

* After every question, talk about what you might say or do. Ask your child for suggestions. Joining in will help them to learn.

* Use the pages at the end of the story to check that your child understands when it is appropriate to use good manners. There's a reward star for every right answer.

* Throughout the day, reward your child's good manners with plenty of praise—and a colorful sticker.

It's fun inside the playhouse.
Teddy wants to go in, too.
But there's no room in
the doorway.

What should Teddy do?

"Excuse me!"

are the words to say.

"Can we come in?"
"Yes, come and play!"

The birthday cake looks yummy.
Bunny wants to try some, too.
But it's very hard to reach
the plate.

What
should
Bunny
do?

"Excuse me!"

are the words to say.

"Can we have some?"
"Yes, you may!"

Vroom, vroom in the go-cart!
Panda's driving, too.
But the road is full of people.

What
should
Panda
do?

"Excuse me!"

are the words to say.

"Can we pass through?"
"Yes. Drive this way!"

It's hard work tidying up the toys.
Dolly thinks so, too.
It would be good to get some help.

What should Dolly do?

"Excuse me!"

are the words to say.

"Can you help me?"
"Right away!"

Everyone's together.
It's a happy day.

The magic words "Excuse me!"
have helped us all to play.

Now it's home time.
It was fun.
But it's time to say "Good night."

Look! Dolly, Bunny, Panda, and Ted got stars for being polite!

What will you say?

If you want to ask a question, what should you say?

If you said "Excuse me" you were right!

If you want to reach across the table, what should you say?

If you said "Excuse me" you were right!

Did you say "Excuse me" in all the right places? Then give yourself four stars!

If you want somebody to move for you, what should you say?

If you said "Excuse me" you were right!

If you want to say something important, what should you say?

If you said "Excuse me" you were right!

I've been polite today!